Fingerprint Owls

and

Other Fantasies

FINGERPR

OTHER

Marjorie

published by
M. EVANS AND COMPANY, INC., New York
and distributed in association with
J. B. LIPPINCOTT COMPANY, Philadelphia and New York

vT Owls and FANTASIES

P. Katz

FOR
HERB

Here's What You Need:

1. an ink pad

2. paper

3. a felt-tipped pen

4. and your fingers

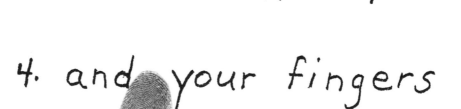

Make Prints With The

tips

pads

sides

of your fingers,

or

with the
side of
your palm

or of your
pinkie,

or the
heel of
your hand.

To make a
tip-first print, ink
the tip part of
your finger and then
the pad part. *To* print,
put tip on paper
first and then,
without lifting
finger from paper,
press pad part down.

A combined pinkie-side-and-palm-side print looks like this:

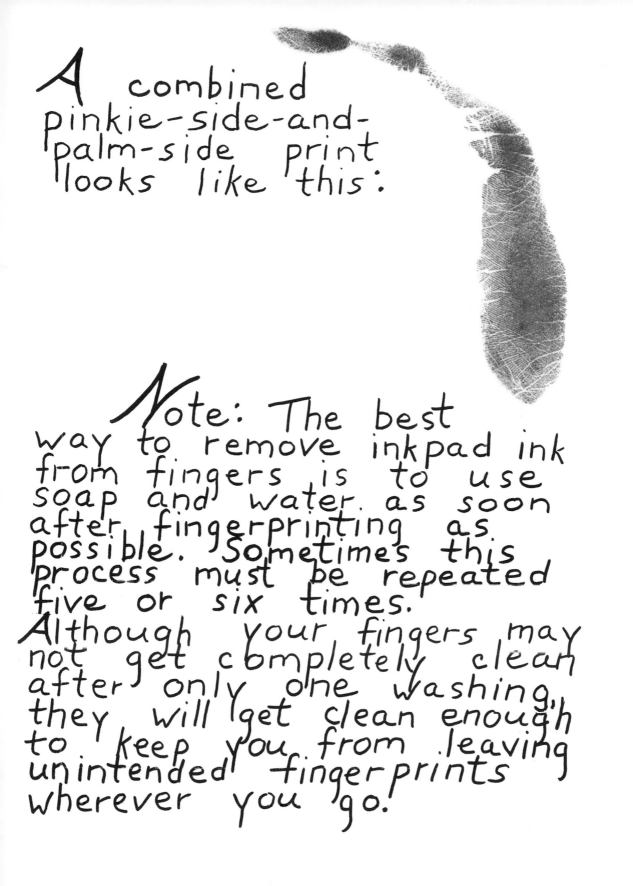

Note: The best way to remove inkpad ink from fingers is to use soap and water as soon after fingerprinting as possible. Sometimes this process must be repeated five or six times. Although your fingers may not get completely clean after only one washing, they will get clean enough to keep you from leaving unintended fingerprints wherever you go.

An Owl

starts with a
tip-first print
made by any
one of the
three middle
fingers.

You can
make three
at a time.

The eyes are
two big dots
in the tip
part of each
print.

Each leg is
a straight line
with three small
lines branching out
at the bottom
to form the
foot.

When
an Owl
sits
on a branch,

its legs
bend
so you
can see
only the feet.

Sometimes they sit

on a roof.

Make a
pad print
horizontally,

add three
easy
triangles,

an eye
and a smile.

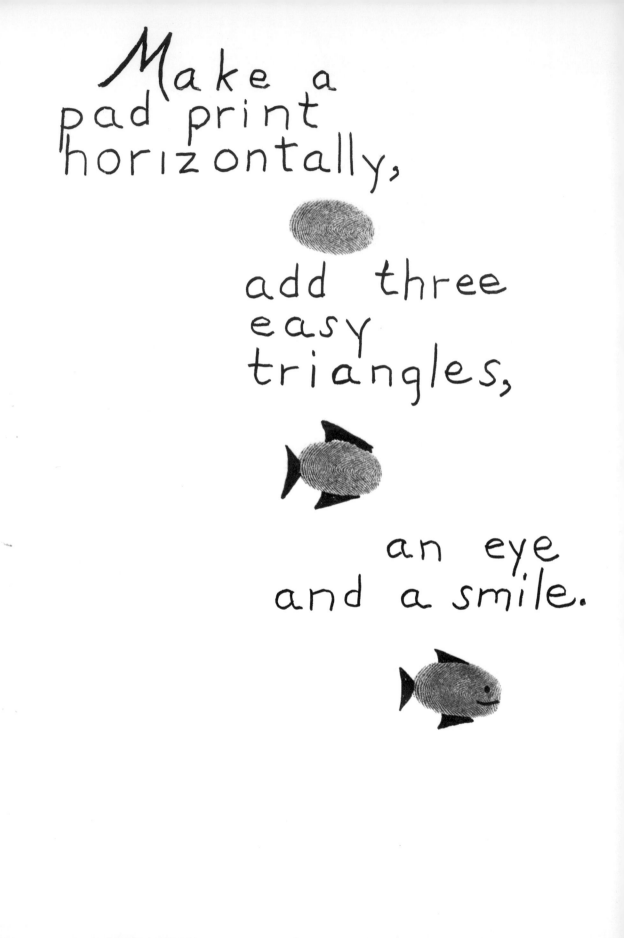

A few squiggles put a whole school of fish in the water.

Make a Mouse

from a
pad print
or
from a
tip print.

Add two c's,
two dots,
six lines
and a squiggle.

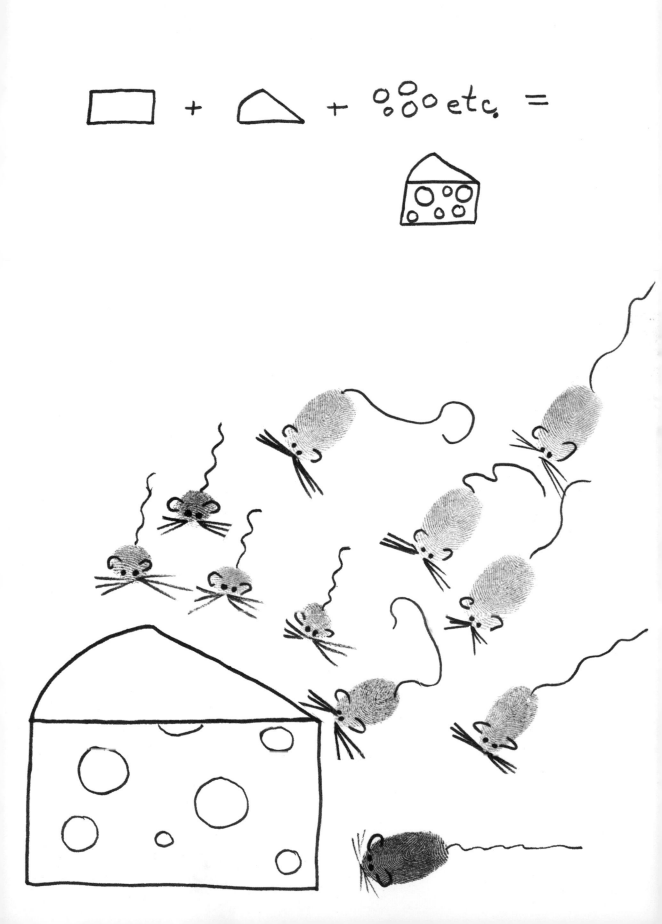

Combine

two pad prints and a side print for a butterfly.

The camel's humps are pad prints; his neck and head are side prints.

And the ducks have tip-print heads on pad-print bodies.

Who's that hiding in the grass?

(To make grass, the tips of four fingers at a time are rubbed in short strokes down the paper.)

(Rabbits, both front and
rear views, start with
tip-first prints.)

Plant a tree...

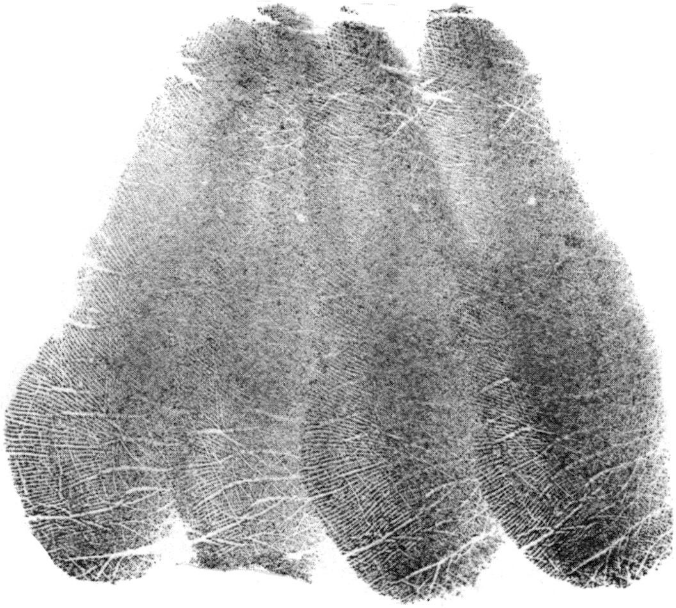

(Build
up the
trunk
with
palm-side
prints,

the branches
with pinkie-
side prints,
and scatter
side-print
leaves.)

and watch it grow!

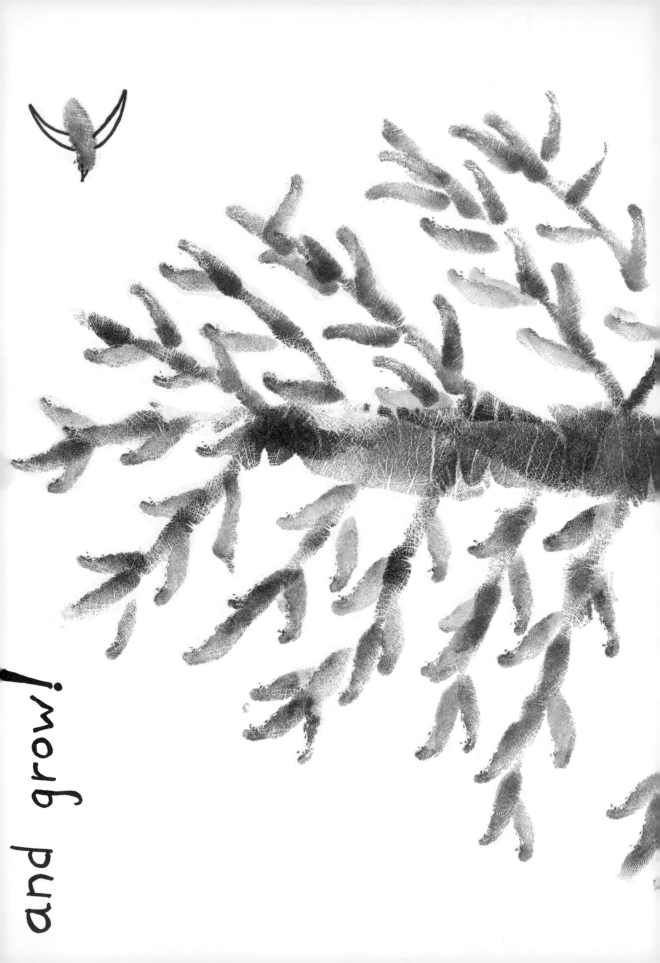

and grow!

A side print,

a few lines and a dot

are all it takes to put
a flock of birds aloft,

or on the  ground.

A few straight lines, curves, dots and triangles

turn pad prints
into a whole
menagerie.

Spiders have two antennae and eight jointed legs set on a tip print.

Lobsters and crabs start with pad prints. Then add legs and claws.

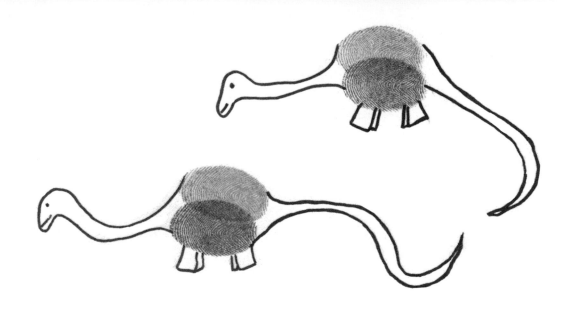

Overlap two horizontal pad prints and add a sinuous neck and tail; short stubby legs and a silly smile finish a fingerprint dinosaur.

A
variety
of prints
creates

a variety of flora.
Experiment with tip,
pad and side prints.
The trunk of the
Saguaro cactus is made
by printing with the
base of the thumb.

A few lines add more variety to your garden. Swirl three figure-8's about the center of a pad print to make a flower.

A few lines and a few props give you a whole cast of characters to play with.

Here are some of the props:

The poodle has a
pad print body, a
side print head, five
tip prints for feet
and tail, held together
by a few short lines.

rah!

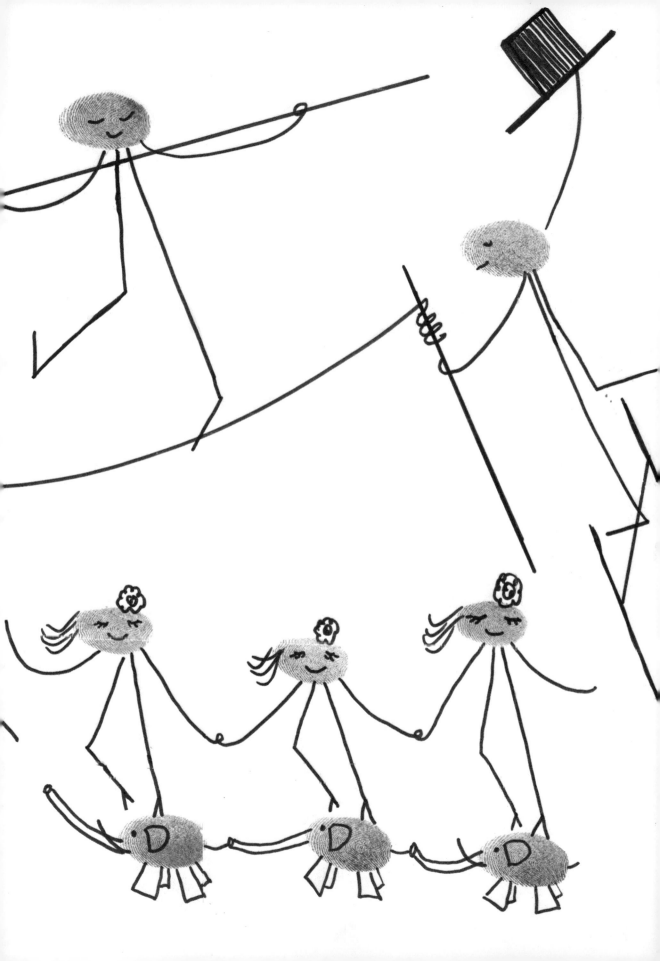

More elaborate pictures can be produced, too. The "Peaceable Kingdom" on the following pages was created with the aid of scissors and rubber cement. First, several fingerprint trees were cut out, positioned and pasted to the background. Fingerprint birds and beasts were cut out and placed on and about the trees. Then some other fingerprint plants were added. Keep cutting and pasting until your picture is complete.

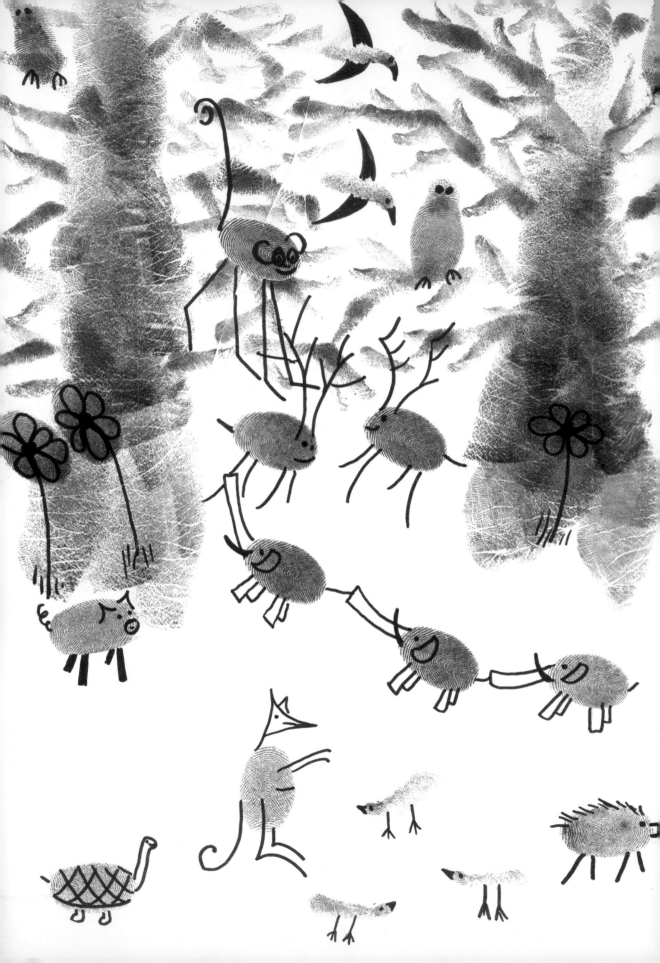

Strips of drafting or masking tape can be used to outline a design. Press tape lightly onto paper. Then fill in the spaces between the taped outline with fingerprints. Remove tapes to uncover your design. The abstract designs on the following pages were made in this way too. Use a variety of prints — tip, side and palm — for more varied effects.

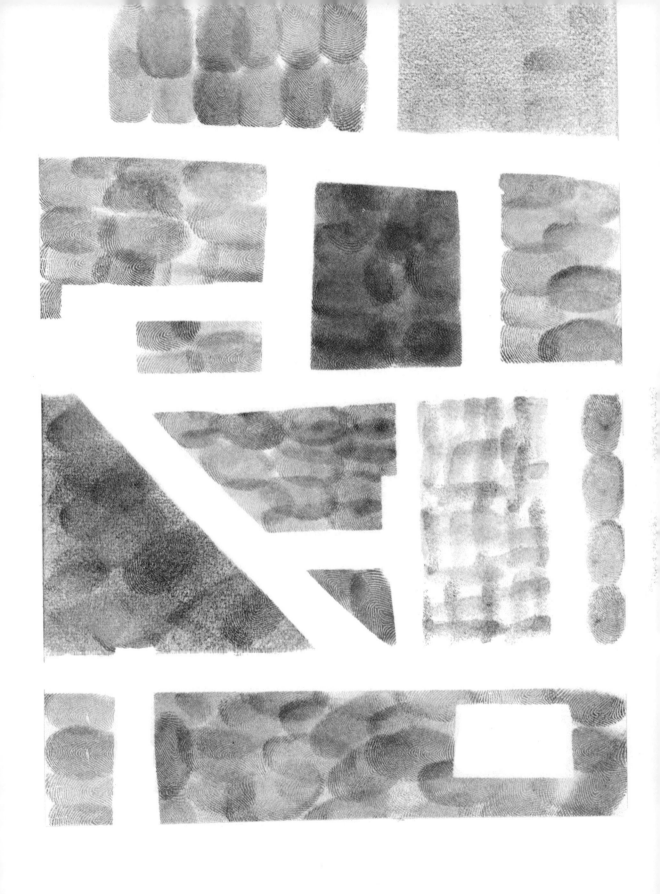

The alphabet uses

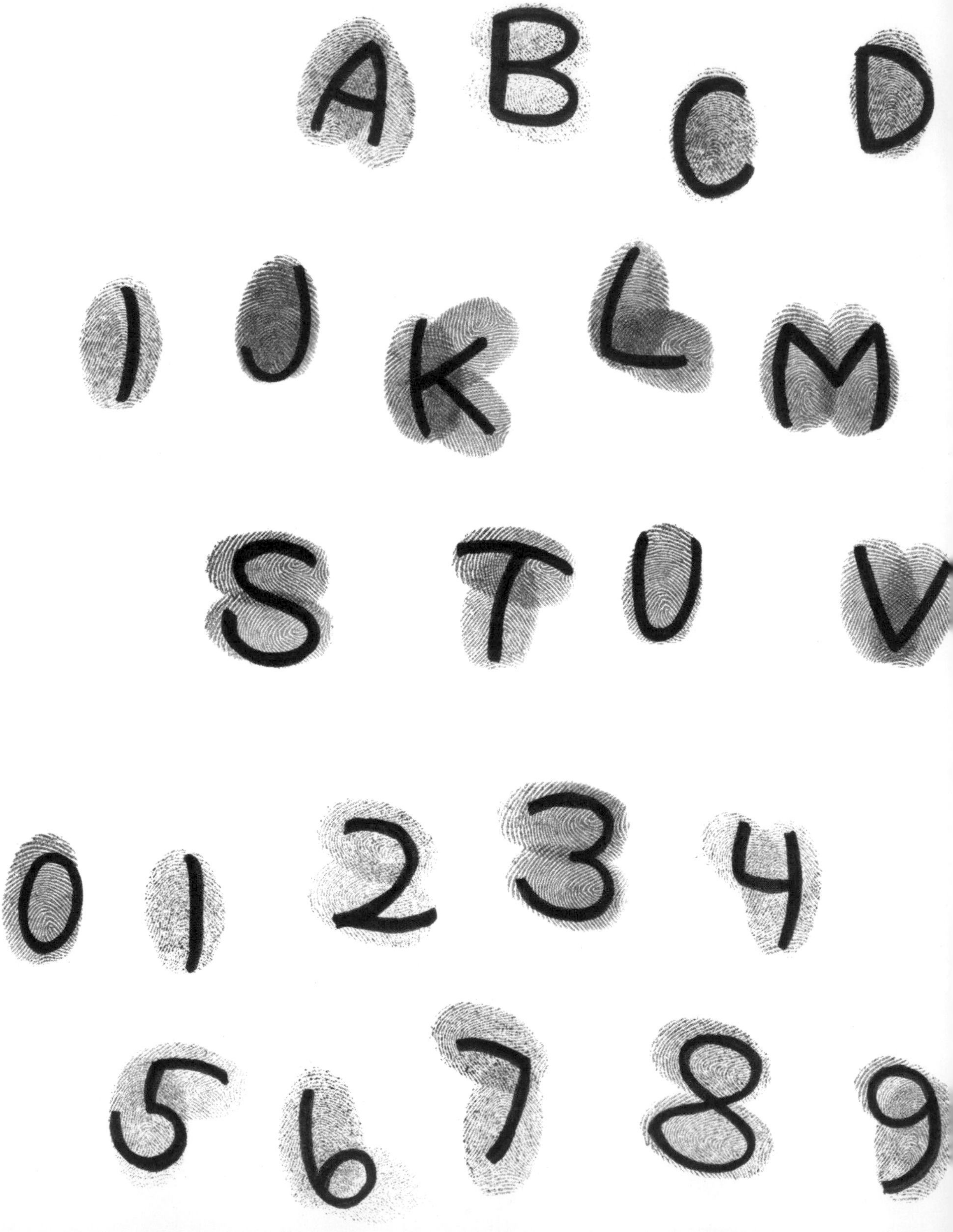

A B C D

I J K L M

S T U V

0 1 2 3 4

5 6 7 8 9

either tip or pad prints.

Things to do with

Patch Your Jeans

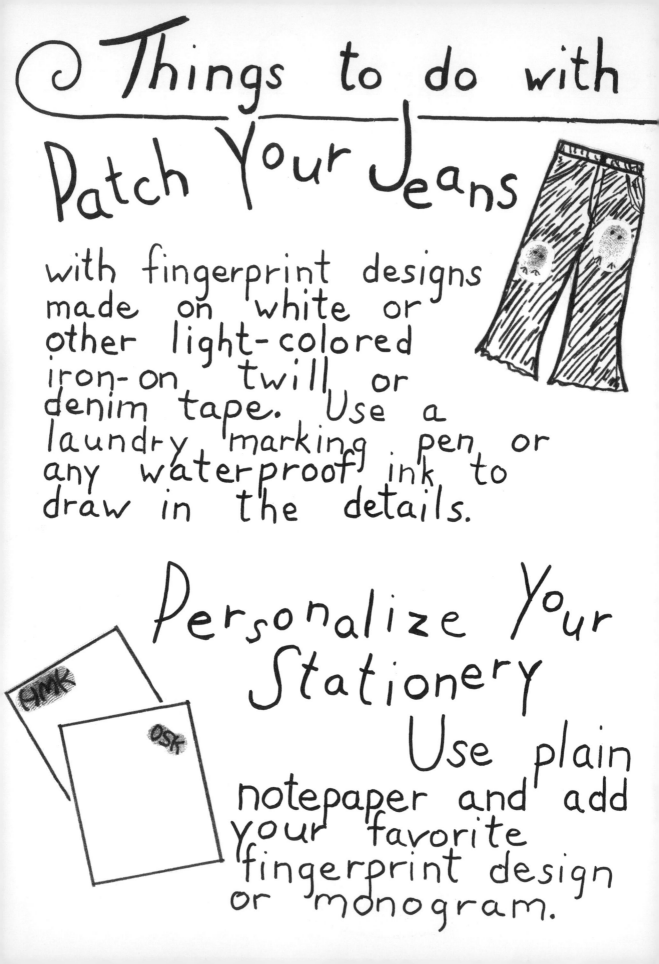

with fingerprint designs made on white or other light-colored iron-on twill or denim tape. Use a laundry marking pen or any waterproof ink to draw in the details.

Personalize Your Stationery

Use plain notepaper and add your favorite fingerprint design or monogram.

Fingerprint Owls:

Print Your Own Distinctive Giftwrap

on tissue paper, rice paper or a roll of shelving paper. Choose a fingerprint design and message suited to the occasion. (Note: On some papers, such as those that are plastic-coated, fingerprints may smear. Use a spray fixative to keep them in their place.)

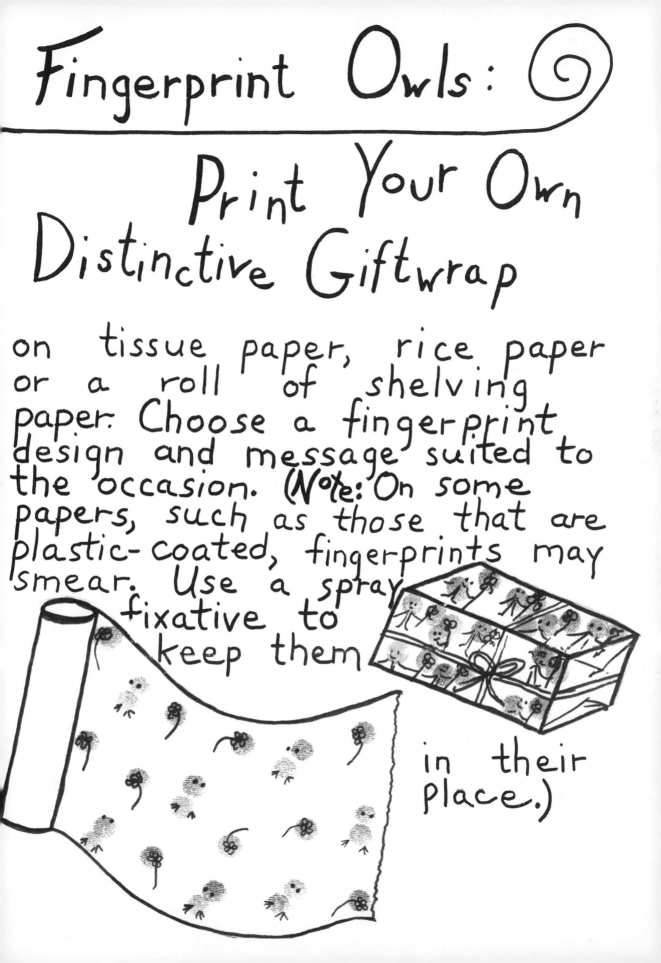

Design Greeting Cards for

birthdays, holidays,

anniversaries and other

special occasions.

Make a Fingerprint Mural

from a roll of shelving paper or a sheet of brown wrapping paper. Use wallpaper paste, white glue or double-faced tape to fasten paper to wall.

Experiment. How many other prints can you think of? What can you do with them?

What about toeprints?

The End